Passive Income
Made Simple

Written By

Dave Bochichio, Founder of Clean Cut Finance

Copyright

Affiliate Link Disclosure

Many links in this book are affiliate links. If you make purchases via these links, Clean Cut Finance may receive a commission. We only recommend products and services we trust.

Table of Contents

What Is Passive Income?

Perhaps one of the most famous quotes about passive income of all time was said by Warren Buffet, who said, "If you don't find a way to make money while you sleep, you will work until you die."

So what is passive income? Passive income is money that you earn regardless of what you're doing. It's residual income that earns itself regularly from things such as something you've made, something you've invested in, or something you're renting out to others. Cutting back your living expenses is also a way to earn passive income because you're essentially earning more by spending less.

We have an article with 40+ ways to cut back your living expenses at:

https://cleancutfinance.com/how-to-lower-monthly-living-expenses/

When you're earning passive income, you're no longer trading time for money, which is what you do when you earn active income. Instead, you're making money even when you sleep. Passive income is a way to reach your financial goals and become financially independent.

INTRODUCTION

Passive income is talked about all over the internet. It's spoken of as the formula to reaching financial freedom. When you earn enough passive income, your job becomes optional. Who wouldn't want that?

I'm not going to go into a long windy story about how passive income changed my and my wife's life (which it did). Instead, I'm going to give you precisely what you came here for.

I present to you Passive Income Made Simple.

You can learn more about the steps of financial independence by going to this article on Clean Cut Finance: https://cleancutfinance.com/what-is-financial-freedom/

Note that passive income generally comes with a lot of work, or significant money, or both. As a result, it's common for passive income streams to take some time to build up.

WHAT ARE THE BENEFITS OF HAVING PASSIVE INCOME?

Passive income is essential for many reasons, and the benefits include:

- Giving you stability in your finances. With regular passive income coming in from multiple sources, if your primary source of income is lost, such as losing your job, you'll have residual income sources to support you while you replace your primary income. The more passive income you have, the less you'll need a paycheck.

- Enough passive income makes you location independent. When you're earning extra income from multiple sources such that you can work less or not at all, you're able to live wherever you want. You could travel for a living, or you could settle down pretty much anywhere, as long as you have the passive income to support it.

- You can retire at a younger age. If you earn a lot of money from passive income, then there's a good chance that you can retire at a younger age. The idea of FIRE, or Financially Independent, Retire Early, is appealing to many, as they don't wish to work for most of their lives.

- You'll be less stressed about your finances. When you have multiple sources of passive income, you'll feel more financially stable and less worried about not having enough money to cover an unexpected expense. Since numerous streams are coming in, others will be there to make up for it if one stops paying off.

  - We talk about reducing financial stress on Clean Cut Finance, and you can read more following this link:

  - https://cleancutfinance.com/reduce-financial-stress/

Passive income simply means more freedom and an easier time with your finances.

DIFFERENT TYPES OF PASSIVE INCOME

When it comes down to it, there are four ways you can earn passive income.

Things That You Buy

Sources of passive income can come from things that you buy. This primarily includes things that you invest in, such as stock, bonds, or hands-off businesses. Anything that you primarily pay money for and then earn passively from is a passive income stream that comes from a purchase.

Things That You Make

You can make things for passive income. This includes creating your own business and running it while earning passively through sales. Creating digital products is another example of passive income because once you've created them, the sales process can be automated, and you can earn for the lifetime of the product.

Things That You Rent

It's possible to earn money simply by renting things you already own, like your car. All you have to do is handle the renting out and returns of your items, and you'll earn by the hour, by the day, by the week, and so on.

Reducing Expenses To Have More Money

Reducing expenses is sometimes called reverse passive income because you're earning by not spending. Apps exist to help you cut expenses, such as Trim, which helps you cut out unused subscriptions and negotiate some of your fixed monthly bills.

How to Create Multiple Streams of Passive Income

Trading your time for money is the typical way most people earn money. But what if you could take that money and your spare time and create one or more streams of passive income.

What would you do with that extra money? Would you save for a big purchase, pay down debt, or fund a significant endeavor?

Money earned from passive income can also be used to create more passive income. When you have passive income-producing more passive income, your monthly earnings continually increase, which means more money in your bank account.

Let's talk about different great passive income ideas that you can choose from to start earning more money.

HOW TO SAVE MONEY FOR PASSIVE INCOME STREAMS

Many passive income streams require some starting capital. Here's how you can begin saving money to get started.

Create a Budget

Often the first thing you can do to save money is to create a budget, as this will help you identify where your money is going each month. Next, determine a weekly savings amount and use that money to create your first source of passive income.

Your first source may simply be an online savings account where you prepare money for another, higher-yielding passive income stream.

You can learn more about creating a budget on Clean Cut Finance at this link:

https://cleancutfinance.com/how-to-create-a-budget/

Cut Back on Living Expenses

By creating a budget, you'll have now figured out where you may be spending too much money. From there, you can lower your expenses by doing things such as:

- Negotiate your cable and internet bills

- Shop around for auto insurance

- Cancel unused subscriptions

Additional, you can find Clean Cut Finance's guide to lowering you rmonthly expenses below.

https://cleancutfinance.com/how-to-lower-monthly-living-expenses/

Increase Your Earnings

You can further earn extra cash to fund more passive income streams by picking up a side hustle. Side hustles range from something you spend a few hours a weekend on to something you do daily after your regular work hours. For example, you might deliver food, do ridesharing, start an online business, or help neighbors around their house.

Clean Cut Finance has an incredibly detailed list of 160+ side hustles you can do to earn more money. Check it out at this link: https://cleancutfinance.com/best-side-hustle-ideas/

Why Is Passive Income Important?

Passive income is important because it allows you to build wealth over time while not trading as much of your time for money. As a result, you'll further reach financial independence and financial security as you gain more passive income.

With enough passive income, work will become optional, which frees you to live your life the way you want.

Passive Income Rating System

Each passive income method is ranked on the following metrics:

- Risk Involved: On a scale of 1 to 10, this rating scores the financial risk of using this method to earn passive income. A 10 means that the method is minimally risky. A rating of 1 means the method is very financially risky. Regardless of rating, make sure to do ample research before starting each passive income method so that you understand what sort of time and money you're putting up.

- Return: This is the expected average return you'll

receive with this passive income method. Because some methods discussed in this book rely heavily on how much money you put in, and some are reliant more on how much time you put in, the return rating is somewhat subjective and based on what I feel how you'll do "on average" if you're successful and in comparison to other methods. Of course, a high return, low feasible (see below) method means you can earn as lot of passive income, but it will be challenging. A return rating of 1 means that you shouldn't expect to earn much money from this method. On the other hand, a return rating of 10 means you should expect to earn a sizeable amount of passive income if you're successful.

- Feasibility: This is the expected difficulty of the passive income method for the average person. A feasibility rating of 10 means just about anyone can do this method. In contrast, a feasibility rating of 1 means that this method can be quite challenging, and a lot of research or technical ability will be necessary to be successful.

- Liquidity: This is how easy it is to liquidate your initial investment if there is a heavy investment portion of the passive income method. For example, if you create a passive income stream mostly with your time and not with a lot of money, then liquidity would be scored 10 or close to 10. However, in the case of buying a business and letting it run passively, liquidity would be lower as selling a business instantly is usually not possible.

- How Passive: This rating determines how passive a method is. A rating of 10 means the method is almost entirely passive and can be left to its own devices almost entirely. A lower rating means you'll need significant involvement before and/or during the building of the passive income stream.

Let's jump into the 41 passive income methods now.

A quick note: I've provided links to many products and services that will enable you to better build passive income. These links are affiliate links and Clean Cut Finance may earn a small commission if you use our links. You are more than welcome to go to a recommended company website without using our links, but do know that I greatly appreciate if you do use our links as it supports making more content like this to help people like you.

1. HIGH-YIELD DIVIDEND STOCKS & FUNDS

Among dividend-paying stocks and funds are those that pay 4% or higher. You don't need to be a personal finance guru to learn how to invest in dividend stocks on the stock market.

Instead, to lower your risk, you can invest in high-yield dividend ETFs. You can do the research yourself or use a tool provided by your investment bank. A stock screener can do wonders.

Read over data that shows the stock or fund's return over one year, three years, and five years. Check to see what the dividend payout has been and if the payout is consistent.

While previous data doesn't imply future returns, you can get an idea of the performance of the stock or fund by doing research this way.

One risk to dividend stock investing that you should know is that a dividend is not guaranteed, and businesses can do poorly or go bankrupt. Therefore, it's always wise to diversify your investments into multiple stocks or a fund that invests in many companies.

Check out Charles Schwab or M1 Finance if you're interested in investing. Both have excellent research tools to help you make informed decisions.

You can sign up for a Charles Schwab account at https://cleancutfinance.com/schwab

Open an M1 Finance account at https://cleancutfinance.com/m1finance

Risk involved: 6: The risk involved in dividend stocks and funds is the capital you invest. In poor market conditions, you could lose some or all of your initial investment, but that said, if you pick good stocks and funds, it's also possible to gain capital on top of the dividends you're receiving.

Return: 5: You'll likely receive somewhere in the ballpark of 3% to 6% from dividends, with some being higher. Because of this, you'll need quite a lot of money to make ample passive income from this one source.

Feasibility: 9: If you find a few good funds, this type of passive income is relatively easy as all you'll need to do is buy more shares periodically. This can even be done automatically.

Liquidity: 9: To get your money back, you would simply sell off all of your shares. You may make a profit or a loss depending on market conditions, however.

How Passive: 10: This method can be fully automated

with automatic transfers and auto-investing.

2. REITS

A REIT is a Real Estate Investment Trust, which are companies that own income-producing commercial real estate. They may own the properties themselves or the mortgages on them.

REITs are required to pay out 90% of their taxable income to shareholders, meaning you often get a much higher dividend return than an average dividend-paying stock.

What's great about REITs is that they provide high dividend yields and moderate capital gains as well. REITs are found on the stock market like other ETFs and funds.

If you don't have the money to invest in your own property or properties, a REIT is an excellent way to break into real estate with less money while also keeping your investment diversified.

Risk involved: 7: The risk here is the chance that the REIT you buy loses value, thus causing you to lose some of your initial investment.

Return: 7: Your returns are based on how much capital you invest. REITs pay out a minimum of 90% of their net earnings in the form of dividends.

Feasibility: 8: Investing in REITs is relatively simple as once you choose one or more REITs to invest in, you can continuously invest money to raise your dividend income.

Liquidity: 7: To redeem your capital, you'll simply sell off all of your shares of the REIT. You may profit or take a loss, depending on market conditions.

How Passive: 10: Once set up, investing in REITs can be completely automated.

3. CROWDFUNDED REAL ESTATE

Similar to buying and renting your own property, crowdfunded real estate allows you to invest with a company like Fundrise with a much smaller amount of money and collect your share of the rent and proceeds of owning real estate, all while Fundrise fully manages everything for you.

This hands-off solution gives you the power of being a landlord without having to do much except invest money and allocate it as you wish.

Investing in crowdfunded real estate can be a long game, and you'll want to make sure you can have your money tied up for a few years or more as you earn regular dividend payments.

Check out Fundrise with this link to get started for as little as a $10 investment:

https://cleancutfinance.com/fundrise

Risk involved: 6: With crowdfunded real estate, your money is illiquid, which means if the properties you invest in lose value, you may not easily retrieve your money until at least a specified amount of time has passed.

Return: 7: Platforms like Fundrise report returns comparable to the stock market while allowing you to diversify your money across dozens of real estate properties.

Feasibility: 9: You can invest with as little as $10 when using Fundrise, and it's almost entirely hands-off. You'll want to read the fine print before investing to ensure this type of investment is right for you.

Liquidity: 4: With crowdfunded real estate, your initial investment may be unavailable to you for at least 5 years, requiring you to pay a penalty if you withdraw before then.

How Passive: 10: Investing in real estate in this manner is almost entirely passive as you simply have to transfer money into your account to get started. The money will allocate automatically. Payouts happen automatically as well.

4. BOND LADDER

A bond ladder is when you purchase several bonds, generally maturing several months apart or one year apart each. So, as an example, you might purchase bonds that mature in 1 year, 2 years, 3 years, 4 years, and then 5 years. When your 1-year bond matures, you receive income, which you can then keep or reinvest into another 5-year bond, which extends the life of your ladder by another year. You can repeat this process indefinitely, gaining passive income each time a bond matures.

Bond ladders generally pay less passive income than other investments like high-dividend stocks, but they're generally considered safer.

In general, a bond ladder produces somewhat predictable, incremental passive income.

Check out Charles Schwab Bank if you're interested in starting a bond ladder to earn passive income.

https://cleancutfinance.com/schwab

Risk involved: 7: A bond ladder can be a relatively safe form of passive income, depending on what type of bonds you invest in. With that in mind, any bond that defaults will result in a loss of capital.

Return: 3: Bonds, while generally safe, don't always produce the best bang for your buck, especially compared to something like dividend investing. That said, bond investing can be more predictable, which may suit people with lower risk tolerance.

Feasibility: 8: A little bit of homework is required to set up a bond ladder, however, it's relatively simple once you do so. Additionally, a financial advisor or investment bank can assist you with setting this up.

Liquidity: 7: You can generally sell off your bond early if you don't want to keep it for the entire term, but this defeats the purpose of a bond ladder and may end up costing you.

How Passive: 9: Once in a while, you'll need to extend your bond ladder, and this is something that is done manually. If you invest in a bond ladder in 1-year increments, then you would have to extend your bond ladder once per year.

5. PEER-TO-PEER (P2P) LENDING

P2P lending is a way to earn passive income by lending other people money. A site like Prosper will allow you to review potential borrowers seeking personal loans for things such as consolidating debt, paying off credit cards, funding a big event, starting a business, paying medical bills, and more.

To minimize risk, you're able to lend as little as $25 per borrower. When you're working with many loans of $25 each, you considerably lower your exposure to one or more loans defaulting, as the interest rates on the other loans will make up for this.

By stacking small amounts of money loaned out, you can create a cash flow of principal and interest coming back to you every month. Rates vary significantly on P2P lending platforms, but you can expect to see in the 4% to 6% range on average, though it's possible to earn more with some strategies.

Peer-to-peer lending performance generally has a low correlation to the stock market, meaning when the market is extra volatile, your P2P account may not be.

Get started with P2P lending at Prosper at https://prosper.com

Risk involved: 4: In P2P lending, if someone defaults on a note, you lose the remaining unpaid balance, making P2P lending somewhat risky. To counter this, investing in dozens or hundreds of notes simultaneously can mitigate loss.

Return: 7: P2P lending returns vary depending on your investment strategy and how often someone defaults on you. While typical results seem to be between 5% and 7%, getting several percent higher or lower is entirely possible.

Feasibility: 6: Investing in P2P lending takes research as you don't want to loan money to simply anyone. Sites like Prosper allow you to create a filter that only shows you notes that meet your exact criteria. With a smart criteria, you're more likely to receive better returns.

Liquidity: 3: Most P2P lending platforms tie up your money for the duration of the loan, less penalties if it's possible to withdraw money early. Prosper, for example, only has notes with 3-year and 5-year terms.

How Passive: 10: Generally speaking, P2P lending platforms allow you to set up automatic investments based on your chosen criteria. This makes this type of investing almost entirely passive. Transfer money into your account, and the platform will do the rest.

6. CERTIFICATES OF DEPOSITS (CDs) OR HIGH-YIELD SAVINGS ACCOUNT

Certificates of Deposit (CDs) and high-yield savings accounts are safe ways to earn passive income as money stored this way is FDIC-insured. While returns for high-yield savings accounts and CDs are very low, currently around 0.5% for many online banks, your money is safer than most other forms of passive income.

With CDs, you'll put your money aside for a set time, and you'll be able to lock in an interest rate to earn. With a high-yield savings account, you can regularly deposit and withdraw money, however, your interest rate may vary each month.

A savings account is an excellent place for an emergency fund, and finding a high-yield savings account will allow your emergency fund to earn a little bit of extra cash for you each month.

An excellent bank to open a CD or a high-yield savings account is CIT Bank. You can open a CIT Bank account at https://cleancutfinance.com/CITSavings

Risk involved: 10: Because CDs and high-yield savings accounts are FDIC-insured up to $250,000, this passive income method is almost entirely safe from loss.

Return: 1: The issue with CDs and savings accounts is that the returns are extremely low. Inflation beats these forms of making passive income which means you're effectively losing money, not gaining. That said, storing money in a savings account for use in emergencies makes perfect sense.

Feasibility: 10: Just about anyone can open up a savings account or get a CD with no trouble whatsoever.

Liquidity: 10 (Savings Account), 5 (CD): With an online savings account, you can withdraw money any time you want, sometimes with a limit to how many times per month. With a CD, you'll usually face penalties if you withdraw your money early.

How Passive: 10: These types of passive income methods earn money on their own. All you need to do is open a savings account or buy a CD.

7. REAL ESTATE RENTAL PROPERTIES

Investing in real estate properties can be a great passive income source. For example, if you're interested in being a landlord, you can buy rental properties - residential or commercial - and collect rent from your tenants. On the other hand, if you want to be more hands-off, you can hire a management company to take care of the property for you. This will reduce your gains a little but allow you to focus more on other things.

Rental income is great because you'll earn predictable monthly payments from each property you have. Of course, you or your management company will have to ensure that you have tenants in each unit and that rent is paid. However, that said, there's great money to be earned in rental properties.

Real estate also appreciates over time, and you have the option to sell your properties for a further profit eventually.

Risk involved: 6: Investing in real estate has risks associated with it, such as property damage, periods of vacancy, tenants not paying rent, and home depreciation if the housing market declines.

Return: 8: Investing in rental properties provides two types of returns. One is the passive income you gain from the rent you collect, and the other is the wealth you accumulate when your properties go up in value, which you can realize when you sell the property.

Feasibility: 6: Real estate investing isn't for everyone, but those who become savvy at it can build a lifetime of passive income. There are a number of books and courses available to educate you in the rental property field.

Liquidity: 6: Selling a house can take time as you may have to wait for a lease to expire and for a buyer to get approved by a bank to make the purchase. Because of this, rental properties are generally not highly liquid.

How Passive: 6: If you become a landlord, you'll need to take care of several aspects of this passive income method. However, you can opt to hire a property management company, which will make this method much more passive.

8. INDEX FUND INVESTING

Unlike mutual funds, which are managed actively by a broker or investor, index funds are passively managed and come with much lower maintenance fees.

What that means for you is that your money will grow faster in a typical index fund as less of your money will be absorbed by fees. So while you may not receive high dividend payouts in some index funds, your money will grow instead.

Index funds that follow the S&P 500 have grown in the 8-10% range on an average year for decades, making them a great place to grow wealth and passive income.

Charles Schwab Bank and M1 Finance are two excellent places to get started with index fund investing.

You can open a Charles Schwab account at :

https://cleancutfinance.com/schwab

Check out M1 Finance at :

https://cleancutfinance.com/m1finance

Risk involved: 8: Index fund investing is a relatively straightforward way to invest in an entire stock market index.

Return: 7: An index fund that follows the S&P 500 historically averages an 8-10% ROI each year, with some years declining and other years being much higher.

Feasibility: 9: It's relatively easy to invest in index funds as all you need is enough money to buy one share of your fund of choice, and this is often under $100.

Liquidity: 7: Generally speaking, you can sell shares of an index fund whenever you want, but you may lose some of your initial investment if the market is trending downward when you make your sale.

How Passive: 10: Index fund investing can be entirely automated, making this a relatively hands-off passive income method.

9. YOUTUBE CHANNEL

YouTube is a competitive place, however, creating excellent videos can earn thousands, if not tens or hundreds of thousands of dollars. Creating how-to videos or reviewing products are two excellent ways to make money on YouTube.

YouTube has ad revenue built-in, but you can also earn money via reviewing products and providing an affiliate link to the product. One or more viral videos where you review or show how to use affiliated products could become a passive income source for years.

Getting started with YouTube generally takes time, and you'll want to learn good YouTube SEO so that viewers can find you.

Aside from YouTube, you can check out TikTok, Twitch.tv, and other streaming websites to make passive money with videos.

Risk involved: 9: Starting a YouTube channel takes very little startup capital. In fact, you might be able to start with just your smartphone and a well-lit room.

Return: 10: A highly successful YouTube channel can bring in over $10,000 per month in passive income, however more realistically, a somewhat successful channel will earn $1,000+ per month.

Feasibility: 3: YouTube is a highly competitive arena, and the majority of YouTube channels fail or don't make much money at all. That said, if you have a profitable niche and make compelling videos that help viewers, you'll significantly increase your chances to do well.

Liquidity: 10: All of the money you make through YouTube is easily cashed out and can be used to upgrade your equipment little by little.

How Passive: 3: To be successful with YouTube, you'll need to continually upload new videos for some time. It can take a year or longer of consistent videos to gain noticeable passive income.

10. ONLINE COURSES

Online education has become incredibly popular over recent years. Websites like Udemy, Skillshare, and Teachable have created platforms for educators to offer online courses to the masses. If you have something you know a lot about and you're able to teach it to others, then creating an online course might make sense.

Online courses are popular in the blogging world, and many blog owners offer courses as one or more of the products that they use to monetize. Once the course is created, the income earned is passive, except for any updates or general upkeep you may have to do on the course - though you may hire out some of this work.

There's no wrong topic to create a course about. Some popular topics we've seen are copywriting, social media management, bookkeeping, DIY projects, drawing, business management, budgeting, programming, and many more. As you can see, the topics fall all over the spectrum, meaning if you're good at something, there may be a need for a course about it.

Udemy can be accessed at

https://cleancutfinance.com/udemy

Skillshare at:

https://cleancutfinance.com/skillshare

Finally, Teachable at:

https://cleancutfinance.com/teachable

Risk involved: 8: Creating an online course takes relatively little upfront money though you may need to pay for a platform to host it, such as with Teachable.

Return: 9: Successful courses have the potential to earn you quite a lot of money, but that said, it can be challenging to create a course that earns you a lot as a lot goes into making and marketing a course.

Feasibility: 4: As mentioned above, creating and marketing a course and building your audience can be truly hit-or-miss. You'll need to do ample research and be somewhat of an expert in your field to be truly successful.

Liquidity: 10: There isn't much to say about liquidity when it comes to online courses. You'll get paid each time you make a sale or at the end of each month, depending on how the platform you host on does payments.

How Passive: 3: Courses generally require some level of commitment from the course creator to make ongoing passive income. You may need to answer emails, do updates, or continually market your course to make sales, for example.

11. BOOKS / EBOOKS

Writing a book or eBook can earn you passive income for years to come. You might pitch your idea to a publisher or self-publish on a site like Amazon.

The best part about books is that they generally have little to no initial investment. That said, if you don't have enough time to write your own book, you could outline it and hire a ghostwriter to write the book for you. Ghostwriters frequently write for authors who don't have the writing skill or time to write their own books.

Books don't necessarily have to be long. Many informative books are short and to the point, meaning that you could pull in recurring income each month if you can write niche books regularly. One strategy is to write short but informative one book every 3-6 months, such as three books per year, and stack your income each year by continually producing more books.

The idea is that each book will serve as its own source of passive income, and you continually create more to buff up your monthly earnings.

Using a tool like Grammarly will improve your writing as

aside from checking spelling and grammar, it betters your writing style, voice, and tone, as well as help you target the type of audience you're writing for. Check out Grammarly here.

Risk involved: 9: Creating a book or eBook costs little to nothing, though you might spend some money on an editor. You may also hire a graphic artist to do a cover design.

Return: 5: Books and eBooks generally don't sell for a lot of money, but if your book is popular or if you write several books, you have the potential to earn quite a lot of passive income from them.

Feasibility: 6: Writing an eBook is not tremendously difficult but writing an eBook that sells well is a bit more challenging. You'll want to do market research and have a solid plan for how you plan on selling it to your audience.

Liquidity: 10: There's minimal startup money involved in writing books and eBooks, giving this method a liquidity rating of 10.

How Passive: 5: I gave eBooks a 5 rating because you will need to keep up with marketing your eBook and possibly writing new ones. If you sell your eBook on Amazon and it gets well known, then this method becomes a lot more passive as you'll have to promote it less often yourself because others will be buzzing about it.

12. Print-on-Demand

Print-on-Demand (POD) is an interesting way to earn money passively. With POD, you sell things like clothes with designs on them or other printed things like journals, towels, shower curtains, wall art, and more. You don't have inventory as each item is printed when the item is ordered, hence print-on-demand.

You can use your own website to show off your shop or use sites like Redbubble to sell.

Companies like Printify will handle all of your printing and shipping needs if you choose your own platform. You simply need to create an account with Printify, upload your designs, position them on the products, and price them out. Then, Printify handles all of the fulfillment. Once everything is set up, you can sell on your own site or on eBay, Etsy, or Shopify.

For more information, head on over to Clean Cut Finance and read our Print-on-Demand tutorial:

https://cleancutfinance.com/make-money-print-on-demand/

If you want to jump right in, you can sign up for Printify at

https://cleancutfinance.com/printify

And if you choose to use Shopify, check out

https://cleancutfinance.com/shopify

Risk involved: 8: There's not much financial risk to starting a POD store because you don't have to buy much upfront except perhaps web hosting and ads if you pursue ads in the beginning.

Return: 5: POD generally has tight margins, and you make money off the sheer volume of sales. If you struggle to make a lot of sales, then your returns will suffer greatly. That said, if you make hit products that your audience loves, you'll have the potential to do really well.

Feasibility: 5: While setting up a POD store can be straightforward enough, you'll still need to come up with designs or hire someone to do so. You'll also need to come up with pricing and a marketing plan. If you decide to do POD for a profitable passive income stream, it may make sense to take a course. We recommend Wholesale Ted's course, which you can find here***

Liquidity: 10: Because you don't hold inventory when you do POD, I rate liquidity at a 10 for this passive income method.

How Passive: 6: POD can be done mostly passively, though you'll need to keep up with things like testing new ads or handling returns. You might also need to switch suppliers if a supplier stops providing something you're selling.

13. Dropshipping

Dropshipping is a process where items are shipped directly from the manufacturer to the customer via a third-party retailer that sells the goods through their website. In short, that means having a website where you sell goods produced by other companies, and you mark it up for a profit.

A popular dropshipping website is https://AliExpress.com, which ships all sorts of products from China. You can pay a fraction of the price for an item on AliExpress and then mark it up on your website for sale to your customers.

Let's take a practical example:

- You find an item on AliExpress that costs $1.75 + $1.20 for shipping, a total of $3
- You list the product for sale on your website for $5
- Your profit is $2, less transaction fees.

From here, you could create a niche online store where you sell to a target audience. Then, as traffic to your online store increases, you make more sales per day, which is completed passively once set up.

Risk involved: 8: Similar to Print on Demand, Dropshipping requires no inventory and very little to start up.

You'll need web hosting, a platform for e-comm, and money for ads.

Return: 4: Dropshipping, like POD, often has tight margins. Depending on what products you dropship, your margins may be even tighter than POD, which hurts your returns. Of course, you may find something worth selling where your margins are greater, which will allow you to make more money.

Feasibility: 5: Dropshipping is relatively easy to set up, but there's a lot of research required to figure out who your audience is, what you should sell them, where to procure the products, and what to price them for.

Liquidity: 10: With no inventory, you won't have to worry about liquidity.

How Passive: 4: Dropshipping requires you to keep up with ads, build an audience, promote to your audience, and ensure your suppliers still have items you're selling and for the same price. You won't need to keep on these things daily, but I rate Dropshipping at a 4 because of these factors.

14. Affiliate Marketing

Affiliate marketing is a great side hustle that can be one of the best passive income ideas if you get enough traction. You can do affiliate marketing through a website, through YouTube, or through sharing on social media.

With affiliate marketing, you'll earn commissions in a variety of ways. You may earn when someone buys something, when they sign up for something, or simply when they click on affiliate links. Signing up for an affiliate network will put you in front of hundreds if not thousands of companies that are looking for publishers like yourself to market their products.

Some affiliate networks require you to be already established, but many will take on newcomers - and most are free to join.

It's best to choose a niche rather than market random things. By selecting a niche, you'll gain a specific audience looking for a particular type of product or service. Your platform will then talk about these products or services, and this will help maximize your earnings.

Once your platform is set up, you'll start earning affiliate income passively.

Popular Affiliate Marketing networks:

- Commission Junction
- Awin
- ShareASale
- Impact
- Rakuten Advertising

For more information on affiliate marketing, head over to Clean Cut Finance for a tutorial on how to make money with affiliate marketing here.

Risk involved: 9: Affiliate marketing requires very little money upfront to get started. You'll need a platform to do affiliate marketing on such as a blog, YouTube channel, email list, or social media.

Return: 10: Successful affiliate marketers can earn over $10,000 per month for their efforts, and this is done somewhat passively once they're established.

Feasibility: 3: While affiliate marketing has a very high potential return, most affiliate marketing websites fail. The trick here is to be consistent and always be learning. Finding a profitable niche and knowing how to build an audience in that niche will be two critical factors to success.

Liquidity: 10: Since very little money goes into making an affiliate marketing website, I give this method a 10 for liquidity.

How Passive: 5: As with any website, you'll have to do

some level of maintenance to keep up with things. You may need to create new content regularly, as well as update old content periodically. You'll need to promote frequently as well.

15. BLOGGING

B logging is an increasingly popular way to make money online. Whether you talk about personal finance, parenting, education, crafts, gardening, or any niche you can think of, there's always an audience out there.

Many bloggers get discouraged after not seeing quick results, and we must remind ourselves that blogging is a marathon, not a sprint. It can often take a beginner blogger over a year to start to earn any significant income, but that said, top bloggers earn a full-time income with their website, making blogging a great way to earn money while living the life you want.

You can earn money from blogging through on-page ads, affiliate marketing, writing sponsored content, and creating your own products and services. As you grow your traffic and your offers, your income will scale up accordingly.

Blogging is something you actively do to build passive income over time. Eventually, you may be able to hire out most of your blogging tasks to turn your income more and more passive.

You can read Clean Cut Finance's beginner guide to how

to monetize a blog at this link:

https://cleancutfinance.com/make-money-blogging/

Risk involved: 9: You can start a blog with just some web hosting. Beyond that, other things that you buy into will make your blogging journey easier and increase profitability. For example, using a service like Grammarly to help you write better will increase the quality of your content, which can help you get more traffic and retain readers.

Return: 10: While less than 1 in 10 bloggers make a full-time income, highly successful bloggers can earn 5-digits per month and more. That said, blogging is a marathon, not a sprint, and it can take years to get to this point.

Feasibility: 3: Starting a blog is relatively simple. Being successful is a whole other story. Approximately 84% of all bloggers never make $100 in their entire time blogging. 5-8% of bloggers make over $10,000 per month. With that in mind, you can see that blogging is a highly variable way to earn passive income if you earn any at all.

Liquidity: 10: Your money isn't tied up in blogging, making this method liquid.

How Passive: 3: Blogging is never truly passive. You'll need to update your content, create new content, and keep up with maintenance tasks. If you're a really successful blogger, you can hire out much of this work, however.

16. CREATING AN APP

If you have coding skills, you may consider creating an app. An app can be something you find on a mobile phone or software used on a computer. Other apps include premium plugins used on websites, paid themes used by WordPress site owners, or games that draw in players.

It makes sense to think outside the box when creating apps because there are many apps out there, and competition can be fierce. Because of this, it pays to find a need that isn't being fulfilled and capitalize on that.

Perhaps you have the capital to invest and an astounding idea but aren't a proficient coder. In this case, you could invest in an app developer and pass on your idea to them to develop. They then develop your app, and you can sell it as your own. Creating a subscription-based model may bring in even more income.

You can hire app developers at sites including:

- Toptal
- Hired
- Upwork

- Dice

Whether you hire out the app development process or you develop your own app, a well-created app that satisfies a need can provide passive income for years to come.

Risk involved: 5: If you create an app from scratch, you may not incur too much financial risk, however, most app developers may need some help from others, including people to test their app, people to help write code, and you'll need to purchase assets if your app has graphics.

Return: 8: Apps can provide a wide variety of returns, including nothing at all, to large sums of money. It'll depend on what your app does and how you market it.

Feasibility: 2: Creating an app requires a lot of technical knowledge or money to hire someone to do it for you. There are a plethora of apps out there, meaning you'll get caught up in the competition. Creating buzz around your app is vital for it to succeed.

Liquidity: 10: You'll get paid regularly when you sell your app, making this quite liquid.

How Passive: 7: Once your app is up and running, this method of passive income is relatively passive. You may need to release bug fixes and patches periodically, but if you're earning enough income, you can hire this work out.

17. INSTAGRAM SPONSORED CONTENT

Gaining a following on Instagram can turn into a semi-passive income strategy that you can capitalize on. Once you've gained a following, you can reach out to brands in your niche to discuss sponsored content. The average micro-influencer can earn between $250-$300 for a sponsored post, whereas someone with over a million followers could earn six digits per year from sponsored content.

Partnering with a brand and including their products or services in pictures and videos you're already creating is a great way to get started. You can also use affiliate links for items in your photos and videos and talk about them in your posts.

Aside from simply sponsored content on Instagram, you can advertise your own products via a link in your bio and then regularly reference your bio in your posts.

While this form of income requires some work, the passive part comes in people finding your profile at different times of the day and earning you money when you aren't actively creating content.

Risk involved: 10: It doesn't cost anything to build an Instagram audience outside of anything you buy to take pictures or things you take pictures of.

Return: 4: While you can certainly make money with sponsored content, the amount you make for the efforts involved are generally less than many other passive income methods.

Feasibility: 5: Building an Instagram audience can be challenging, but that said, once you get to over 1000 followers, it's entirely possible to start earning money by linking up with brands in your niche.

Liquidity: 10: There's no money tied up when you're an Instagram influencer.

How Passive: 3: This method isn't as passive as others. You'll need to make new sponsored constantly. What is passive is that once you build up an audience, you'll have to hustle a lot less to earn more money since brands will pay you more for having a larger, more engaged following.

18. STOCK PHOTOGRAPHY

Stock photography is used all around the world on various forms of media for all kinds of companies. If you excel at photography, you can sell your photos on stock photo image sites like https://iStockPhoto.com

At stock photo sites, you're paid a commission every time your stock photo is downloaded. As an excellent photographer, you could upload dozens of pictures over time, ranging from landscapes to typical office pictures to people sitting around with each other and more, and turn that into a lucrative passive income side hustle.

A site like iStockPhoto also has a section for illustrations, so if photography isn't your strong point, but you're skilled at sketching, you can make similar money with stock illustrations.

Risk involved: 7: You'll need a decent camera and lighting to take stock photography that actually sells. For professionals, you might also need to pay people to pose in specific situations, such as a group of professionals reviewing a presentation, if you were to take business-related stock photos.

Return: 3: Stock photography doesn't usually pay very

well per download, however, if you've taken many photos that do well, your earnings are almost entirely passive, meaning that even though your returns might not be extraordinary compared to other methods, you'll be able to sit back and collect.

Feasibility: 7: It takes skill to take photography worthy of stock photos, but once you get started, you can often sell dozens of similar photos on websites on istockphoto.com***

Liquidity: 10: The money you earn from stock photography is easily collected on a regular basis.

How Passive: 10: You may want to continue taking photos to increase your portfolio, but once your photos are uploaded, this method of passive income is almost entirely passive.

19. Printables

Printables are trendy on Etsy and can fall into a wide variety of niches. Some popular printable niches include:

- Budget planners
- Fitness trackers
- Home chore trackers
- Calendars
- Checklists
- Studying notes
- Personal goals and progress

Whether you do your own graphic design for your printables or come up with a rough draft and hire out the professional design, you can earn passive income selling your printables on Etsy or your own website.

One great thing about printables is that many people use them, each with their own preferences. That means even if a particular type of printable is saturated, you may be able to wiggle into the market by providing something that your competition doesn't, whether by something on the actual printable or via the actual design.

Risk involved: 10: Creating printables is something you

can do for free or for a very low cost. You can also consider hiring a graphic designer to design the printables for you with a commercial reselling license.

Return: 5: Printables can be a great source of passive income, though I rated them at a 5 because of the competition. While you can earn $1,000 per month or more selling printables, you'll need to really narrow in on your audience and promote effectively.

Feasibility: 6: Creating printables is relatively easy. Where you'll find a challenge is setting yourself out from your competition and building an audience.

Liquidity: 10: You won't have your money tied up when you sell printables.

How Passive: 7: A well-established printable store can be run mostly passively. You may have to deal with customers once in a while, and you'll undoubtedly want to promote your store regularly.

20. RENT YOUR HOME

Have a spare bedroom? Use a site like https://Airbnb.com to rent out your spare room to people staying in your area.

If you live in a trendy area, you could make up to $1,000 or more per month renting out rooms.

A popular use of Airbnb is to own a vacation rental property and use Airbnb to rent it out during peak months. For example, perhaps you have a home in a lake community that is popular for tourists during the summer or a home in the mountains that's popular during ski season. One idea is to rent out weeks or weekends to tourists and hire a company to clean up between guest stays.

Risk involved: 7: Renting out a room in your home is generally not too financially risky, though you may have to deal with an occasional renter who damages your property.

Return: 6: If you live in a touristy area, you can potentially make quite a bit of near-passive income renting out one or more rooms in your home.

Feasibility: 8: If you have a house with a spare room and live in an area where people need a place to stay, such as in a touristy area, then this way of earning semi-passive income may be right for you.

Liquidity: 10: Your money isn't tied up when you use this passive income method.

How Passive: 3: You'll need to prepare your spare room for each new renter, and you'll likely need to interact with the renter at some point, making this form of passive income less passive.

21. RENT YOUR CAR

———◆———

D o you have an extra car or aren't using your car regularly? On a website like https://turo.com, you can rent your car to people in your area. A quick lookup shows you can earn around $80 and upward of $250 a day or more, based on the type of vehicle you're renting.

This is an excellent way to earn some extra income passively. If you rent through Turo, you can get insurance directly from their provider so that you don't have to worry about what happens in case your renter damages your car. The average person renting one car earns just over $10,000 per year.

Risk involved: 7: Renting out your car has a similar risk to renting out a room in your house. Websites where you list your car, have insurance options to protect you if someone damages your car, but damage to your car can still cost you other ways, such as not having a vehicle when you need it.

Return: 6: It's possible to earn $100 a day or more renting your car if you live in an area where cars are regularly needed.

Feasibility: 8: Just about anyone with a car can rent out their car if they don't need it in the interim. That said, you'll need to live somewhere where it's convenient to meet potential renters.

Liquidity: 10: Your money isn't tied up when you rent out your car.

How Passive: 6: You'll need to maintain your car between renters, and you'll have to interact with customers when they pick up and drop off. Aside from that, this method of earning passive income is fairly passive.

22. Rent Out Your Garage

Similar to renting out a room in your home, you can rent out your garage to someone who needs a place for their extra stuff or to park their car. This can be especially good in the winter months for people who have nice cars that they want to keep safe from the snow or other inclement weather.

https://neighbor.com is a site that lets you list your garage for rent to people needing a short or long-term parking spot. The website reports that you can earn between $200 and $400 per month, mostly passively, simply by renting out a parking spot in your garage.

Risk involved: 8: Renting out your garage doesn't put you at much financial risk unless the person renting from you does something to damage your garage, which is still likely less financially risky than renting out your car or a bedroom in your home.

Return: 3: You might not make a whole lot of money renting out your garage, but it's relatively easy to do so if you're not using your garage for anything else.

Feasibility: 8: Just about anyone with a garage can rent it out to someone nearby who needs the extra space.

Liquidity: 5: I rated this at a 5 because if you rent month-to-month, you might not be able to easily have someone remove their belongings from your garage immediately, as you may have to wait till the end of the month, similar to if you were renting a house or apartment to someone with a lease.

How Passive: 9: Renting a garage out is mostly passive once you get someone in there. You likely won't have to deal with the renter all too much, except to collect payment each month or if they have a request.

23. ADVERTISE ON YOUR CAR

S ome companies will pay you to let them advertise on your car. You'll be sent ads to place on the sides, front, or back of your car and paid to simply drive normally.

At https://carvertise.com, you can earn between $350 and $1500 per advertising campaign, which averages $100-$300 per month, simply by wrapping your car in advertisements.

This is an excellent option for commuters to earn money day-to-day, which can cover gas and car maintenance costs, leaving you more money each month for other things.

Risk involved: 10: You won't need to put money up for this form of passive income as you'll be directed by the company as to where to bring your car to get your car professionally wrapped with advertisements.

Return: 2: While this passive income method is relatively easy to do, as it mainly requires driving as you usually do, you generally won't earn a ton of money doing it, compared to how much you can earn with other methods. That said, you can still expect to earn up to $300 per month when using your car as an advertising tool.

Feasibility: 9: If you have a car, live in an area that's supported, and meet all other criteria, then this method is relatively easy to earn passive income.

Liquidity: 10: You won't put any money upfront for this passive income method.

How Passive: 8: Because you're already driving around as you usually do, this method gets a rating of 8 because you won't be doing much else out of the ordinary except getting your car wrapped and unwrapped periodically.

24. LICENSE MUSIC

You've heard of stock photos, but how about stock music? Songs and jingles are needed for common media such as commercials, videos, apps, and more. So instead of getting signed for your music, what if you sold stock music instead?

Listen to music found in typical shows, YouTube videos, and mobile games you play, and then compose your own music.

License your music on sites such as https://audiojungle.com or https://pond5.com. By doing this, you can start earning money from your music without having to break into the music industry.

Risk involved: 7: You may need to buy specialized equipment to make music worthy of the kind of income you're hoping to achieve. This includes software, instruments, hardware, and digital samples.

Return: 4: Popular stock music can earn you quite a bit of money, but it can be tough to break into this field. If you work with a private buyer, you can often earn quite a lot more money, though this causes your income to be less passive as you'll likely be unable to license your music to other buyers.

Feasibility: 5: This type of passive income stream is generally reserved for skilled musicians, making it challenging for just about anyone else to get involved. There's also quite a bit of competition between musicians to make money with this stream.

Liquidity: 5: Getting back your initial investment if things don't work out might be tricky, which is why I give this method a 5 liquidity rating.

How Passive: 8: Once you've uploaded any number of tracks to a stock music site, this method of passive income is mostly passive, though promoting your songs will help you earn more money.

25. Cashback Apps

An interesting form of passive income is apps that pay you to spend money. That may seem counterintuitive, but if you're already going to buy something online, wouldn't it be nice to get a percentage of that money back?

An app like Honey offers discount codes at many online retailers, and you'll also earn Honey Gold when you shop. Honey Gold can be converted into cash or gift cards when you reach $10 worth or more.

Swagbucks is a more expansive app that allows you to earn cashback from scanning your receipts, shopping online, and trying out products and services.

For grocery stores and retailers, check out Ibotta to start earning cashback whenever you shop for specific items.

When you combine multiple cashback apps, you can earn quite a bit just for shopping like you usually do.

Check out Honey at https://cleancutfinance.com/honey

Sign up for Swagbucks at

https://cleancutfinance.com/swagbucks

Lastly, you can check out Ibotta at:

https://cleancutfinance.com/ibotta

Risk involved: 10: Using cashback apps generally has no financial risk as you're earning money from the money you'd be normally spending.

Return: 1: You'll often earn 1-5% cashback on qualifying purchases, which may not seem like much, but it can certainly add up over several months or an entire year.

Feasibility: 10: Anyone with a smartphone can use a cashback app.

Liquidity: 10: There's no money tied up when using a cashback app though you may need to earn a minimum amount before getting paid out.

How Passive: 9: You'll earn money every time you scan your receipt or purchase via the app, making this method almost entirely passive.

26. CASHBACK CREDIT CARDS

S ome credit card companies pay you in the form of cash and rewards for using their cards. If you frequently use credit cards to pay for everyday purchases and bills, getting a cashback credit card may make sense.

You may find yourself earning a base of 1% cashback with higher percentages for specific purchases. For example, some cash back cards specialize in things like gas, travel, groceries, and more.

Now, when you swipe your card, you're earning a little bit of passive income sent back at you.

Two credit cards that currently offer great cashback rewards are the Chase Freedom Unlimited card and the Citi Custom Cash card.

Risk involved: 10: Technically speaking, the only financial risk with this passive income method is spending more than you usually would in order to collect cashback, which would defeat the purpose.

Return: 1: You'll generally earn 1-5% cashback on qualifying purchases.

Feasibility: 10: Anyone with a credit card can use this method.

Liquidity: 10: No money is tied up with this passive income method though you may need to earn a certain amount of cashback before cashing out.

How Passive: 10: You'll earn money whenever you swipe your credit card, making this method entirely passive.

27. VENDING MACHINE BUSINESS

Perhaps a less common but interesting way to earn passive income is with a vending machine business. This income is not entirely passive unless you hire someone to do maintenance work such as restocking the machine.

That said, a vending machine business can provide steady passive income. You'll pick a location and what to sell, and then you or someone you hire takes care of day-to-day operations. You might sell coffee, sandwiches, soda, candy, or non-food items. There are lots of things to choose from.

Note that this form of semi-passive income is a business, and you'll have some startup costs and risks involved.

Below is a link to a guide from NerdWallet to starting a vending machine business.

https://www.nerdwallet.com/article/small-business/how-to-start-a-vending-machine-business

Risk involved: 3: A vending machine business, while carrying the possibility of being quite lucrative, can cost a lot of money to startup and cost a lot if your business ends up not working out.

Return: 9: The potential return for a successful vending machine business is quite high. You'll simply need to keep the operation going or hire someone to manage it.

Feasibility: 5: Vending machine businesses cost a bit to startup and it'll take some knowhow to keep it running, but that said, it can be a great business venture.

Liquidity: 5: If your business begins to slide, you may need to find someone to buy your vending machines or your business as a whole.

How Passive: 6: A successful vending machine business hires out most of the work, which makes this passive income method somewhat passive once it's up and running.

28. STORAGE RENTALS

A storage rental business can be a lucrative way to earn passive income. Typically, you can make $75 to over $500 per month for each unit. However, this type of business does have a high cost of entry, and you can expect to spend over $25,000 to get started.

With that in mind, if you live somewhere with a high need for storage, you can corner the market and earn a fair share of money each month simply by renting out space.

You'll need land and money to cover building the units. You'll make decisions like offering basic units or climate-controlled storage units, as well as the size of units and number of units.

You can find further information on starting a storage rental business at Don't Work Another Day's website:

https://www.dontworkanotherday.com/storage-unit-rental-business

Risk involved: 1: It's typical to spend over $25,000 to get started with a serious storage rental business, so it's critical to do all of your research before getting involved.

Return: 10: Despite the significant investment to get involved in this type of business, you have the potential of earning a full-time income that's mostly passive once you're set up.

Feasibility: 3: This type of business requires a significant financial investment and a bit of know-how to ensure that you're going to be successful. You'll likely need to hire staff, buy or rent land, and take care of all the logistics for setting everything up.

Liquidity: 3: If your business turns south, you'll have trouble getting back your initial investment unless you find another entrepreneur who's interested in taking over. Depending on where you live, this may be challenging to pull off.

How Passive: 7: While a lot goes into creating a storage rental business, once you hire staff to run it, it can be run mostly passively. You could even run this business almost entirely passively if you hire a trusted manager to take care of day-to-day operations and simply cut you a check each month.

29. ROBO-INVESTING

When you use Robo-investing, an algorithm allocates your money for you based on the financial goals that you provide it.

Robo-advisors have become increasingly popular in recent years, though they should not replace getting sound investment advice from a financial advisor should you have financial questions and concerns.

That said, through Robo-investing, you may be able to up your returns and earn passive income without having to think much more about it except for determining your initial goals and investing money regularly.

Check out M1 Finance to get started with Robo-investing.

https://cleancutfinance.com/m1finance

Risk involved: 8: Robo-investing is a relatively safe way to invest your money as the Robo advisors algorithm will handle all of your investment choices. As with any investment, it's possible to lose money, but you'll average gains over the long term in most conditions.

Return: 4: Your return will be dependent on how much

you invest, however, typical Robo-advisors report an average of 5% return on investment.

Feasibility: 10: Just about anyone can get started investing with Robo advisors.

Liquidity: 7: You may lose money, as with any stock market investment, when you invest with Robo advisors, which is why I give this a 7 liquidity rating. With this in mind, Robo-investors are usually somewhat safe when compared to picking stocks on your own.

How Passive: 10: Robo-investing can be fully automated, meaning you can earn passive income regularly by simply setting it up.

30. REFINANCE YOUR STUDENT LOANS

Refinancing student loans at a lower interest rate means you're paying less money each month. This is a reverse form of passive income, meaning you're saving money that you usually spend.

By paying less, you'll have more money coming into your bank each month, which is a form of passive income in itself.

Check out https://sofi.com to get more information on refinancing your student loans.

Risk involved: 8: It doesn't cost anything to refinance your student loans, however, one financial risk is that you may lose access to income-based repayment plans.

Return: 2: You earn reverse passive income when you refinance your student loans because you save money on interest payments. The amount you save will be based on your current interest rates and terms and your new loan's interest rates and terms.

Feasibility: 8: Many people with student loans have the option to refinance them. People on income-based repayment plans may choose not to do this method as it may cause them to lose access to their plans.

Liquidity: 10: You can pay off your student loans whenever you're able to afford to.

How Passive: 10: Refinancing your student loans offers immediate and long-term savings that are entirely passive.

31. MAKE MONEY WATCHING TV

Watch a lot of TV? Would you like to be paid to watch shows?

When you join Nielsen, you can earn free gifts just for watching TV and other streaming devices.

Not everyone is selected, and you'll have to agree not to disclose that you're part of the Nielsen family. However, if you become part of the team, you'll get occasional gifts just for watching everyday TV.

Read more about joining the Nielsen family here:

https://www.nielsen.com/us/en/about-us/panels/ratings-and-families/

Risk involved: 10: There is no notable financial risk involved in watching TV for money.

Return: 1: You may earn very little or simply only gifts for watching TV.

Feasibility: 2: Very few people are invited into the Nielsen program and similar programs where you're paid to watch TV.

Liquidity: 10: No money is tied up with this passive

income method.

How Passive: 10: This method is entirely passive, as long as you're sitting on the couch watching TV like you usually do.

32. Laundromat Business

Another interesting source of passive income is a laundromat business. In the case of owning a laundromat business, you earn passive income for each washer and dryer machine you own.

Many laundromat businesses can be bought as they currently stand, meaning less work for you, as long as you have the money to buy into the business and optionally have someone to work with who can help you with day-to-day tasks.

This is a more advanced form of passive income and requires doing some due diligence. You'll want to determine your startup and upkeep costs as well as figure out if the business will be profitable.

That said, a profitable laundromat business is relatively hands-off and can earn you a nice chunk of change each month.

Risk involved: 1: A lot of money is required to start up a laundromat business, and failing to maintain the business could cause you to lose significant capital.

Return: 8: You'll earn money from each machine you

own and mostly passively, especially if you hire someone to manage everything.

Feasibility: 5: This business requires some know-how and a financial investment to get started.

Liquidity: 5: If your business goes south, you may need to find another entrepreneur to buy all your business, else you'll be left figuring out how to sell all of your machines, potentially at a loss.

How Passive: 10: This business is entirely passive if you hire someone to handle day-to-day tasks. Otherwise, you may need to stop by periodically to check on things or answer customer inquiries via phone or email.

33. INSTALL APPS ON YOUR PHONE

You can earn passive income just by using your phone regularly or by shopping from it.

For example, with Swagbucks, you can earn passive income by watching ads, shopping online, and scanning your receipts. There's also the Swagbucks search engine where you'll earn money just for searching the internet.

Trim is an app that identifies subscriptions that you may be paying too much for or are no longer using. It also helps you b negotiating your cable, internet, and phone bills for you. Trim earns you reverse passive income by saving you money every month that you had been spending beforehand.

Acorns is a round-up app that rounds up all transactions to the nearest dollar and automatically invests the extra money. You can select your investment strategy, and Acorns does the rest. Plans start as little as $3 per month.

You can sign up for Swagbucks at:

https://cleancutfinance.com/swagbucks

Check out Trim at

https://cleancutfinance.com/asktrim

And, more info on Acorns can be found out:

https://acorns.com

Risk involved: 10: Apps that pay you for being installed on your phone don't (or shouldn't) cost you anything.

Return: 1: You likely won't earn much from this passive income method, but it's straightforward to take part.

Feasibility: 10: Just about anyone with a smartphone can do this method.

Liquidity: 10: No money is tied up in this passive income method.

How Passive: 10: For many apps, you'll earn money simply by having the app installed on your phone. Some apps may require some interaction at times.

34. WRITE AND SELL PLR CONTENT

If you're a writer, a passive income idea is to write and sell PLR content. PLR stands for Private Label Rights and what that means is that you'll be writing articles that you can sell to multiple other websites.

With PLR content, you write one article and sell it repeatedly to many website owners, and they will edit the article as their own to better fit their needs. You might sell an article for $3 each, depending on the length and the type of article, but you might sell that $3 article to dozens of businesses. This can be done passively once the article is written.

The key to earning passive income with this technique is to write high-quality articles and then find a platform to sell them repeatedly, such as in Facebook groups for bloggers. You can also place them on your own blog or e-commerce store.

Risk involved: 9: Generally speaking, the only financial risk you incur when writing and selling PLR content is any tools you use to write better content, such as Grammarly to improve your writing or an SEO toolkit.

Return: 4: PLR content pays a lot less than freelance

writing and ghostwriting, however, since you can sell the same piece of content multiple times, it can be somewhat passive.

Feasibility: 7: If you have a knack for writing, or if you're someone who has the passion for improving your writing, then you should have the ability to write and sell PLR content.

Liquidity: 10: Money isn't tied up in this passive income method.

How Passive: 4: You'll likely have to continually write content to improve sales. You'll also need to market your content. That said, after some time, this method becomes more passive.

35. Selling Digital Artwork on Etsy

Selling digital artwork on Etsy is an excellent passive income idea for artists looking to make money on their drawings, paintings, and other works.

There are many ways to sell digital artwork, and Etsy is a popular way to do it. Etsy is a great place to start selling your artwork because of how much traffic the site gets and how easy it is to set up a shop.

Etsy is free to use, and you can set your own prices. People trust Etsy, which means you don't have to create a website to sell your art and worry about people not trusting the payment process.

Risk involved: 9: The financial risk involved with this passive income method comes down to anything you spend in order to create the digital artwork and any ads you might use to get traffic to your Etsy store.

Return: 3: It's difficult to rate this passive income method as digital artwork has a wide variance in pricing, coming down to how the artwork will be used. I rated it as a 4 if you are truly successful in this field.

Feasibility: 4: Selling digital artwork is competitive and requires a lot of talent to wow your audience.

Liquidity: 10: No money is tied up in this passive income method.

How Passive: 6: After you've created a portfolio, most of your selling becomes passive, except for you promoting your store and your artwork. Having a website can help with this.

36. FLIPPING WEBSITES

This semi-passive income idea involves buying existing websites and selling them for a profit at a later date. You can buy and sell websites on Flippa.

The website you purchase should have good content, a large audience, and making some income already. It is recommended that you spend some time improving the website before selling it.

While improving the website, you'll likely earn passive income from it as the website may be monetized with methods like ads, affiliate marketing, and products for sale.

Start this semi-passive income stream at

https://cleancutfinance.com/flippa

Risk involved: 3: When you buy a website, you risk not being able to sell it for a profit. Websites range in prices, all the way from several hundred dollars to over a hundred thousand dollars.

Return: 10: Provided you significantly improve the website you're flipping, you can make a fortune flipping websites.

Feasibility: 5: You'll need to know what you're doing to do this passive income method. If you're a blog flipper, for example, you'll need to know how to significantly increase traffic and revenue so that you can sell your newly acquired blog to the next owner.

Liquidity: 5: If the website you buy ends up losing traction, you could lose significant money when you sell it off. That said, the opposite is true, too, if the site improves.

How Passive: 3: You'll likely need to put in a lot of work to improve a site to make it worth the flip. That said, you can also collect semi-passive income from the site while you're working on it.

37. BUYING AND SELLING DOMAINS

Another semi-passive income idea is to buy and sell domains. In order to make money with this method, you'll want to buy or register domain names that you feel will become more valuable in the future.

Names that include catchy phrases or potential business names can be very valuable in the future because they're easy to remember and may be desirable to someone one day.

.com sites are by far the most valuable domain extensions because they're the most well-known.

The best way to find potential domain names is to use a domain name registrar. These companies will let you search for domain names by keyword, extension, or TLD (top level domain).

Check out Namecheap to register your domain names at the best prices.

https://cleancutfinance.com/namecheap

Risk involved: 8: Your financial risk is the annual charge of the domains you buy and hold on to until you find someone to sell them to. This is generally pretty affordable, especially if you go with Namecheap, where you can hold domains for under $25/year.

Return: 5: While you can make a lot of money auctioning off domains, you may make no money at all. This leaves a significant variance in how much you can earn with this method.

Feasibility: 7: This method is relatively simple to do though you'll need to think of domain names to register that you feel someone will want in the future and for a fair share of money.

Liquidity: 5: You can only sell a domain if you have an interested buyer. Otherwise, you'll have to let it expire and lose your entire investment.

How Passive: 9: After you've purchased a domain, you can simply wait for someone to buy it from you, or you can find interested parties yourself.

38. SELLING WORDPRESS THEMES

If you've got talent at web design, one form of passive income is creating and selling one or more WordPress themes. Some themes allow users to buy and customize them and rebrand them as their own. In this case, you can take a customizable theme and make your own version of it, and from there, sell it to bloggers and webmasters.

You'll need to know how WordPress themes work and how to create or customize them. This is a skill that you can develop simply through practice.

https://TemplateMonster.com is a great site to sell WordPress themes.

Risk involved: 9: The financial risk involved in selling WordPress themes is any money you spend to help you make the themes or the money spent on ads to market them.

Return: 5: A basic custom WordPress theme can be sold for up to a few hundred dollars, but a premium custom business theme can go for several thousand.

Feasibility: 5: You'll need technical and design know-how to make a stunning WordPress theme worth selling. This field is also reasonably competitive as established themes are out there already.

Liquidity: 10: Money isn't tied up in this passive income method.

How Passive: 8: If you're creating basic WordPress themes that can be mass distributed, then this method is a lot more passive once you've created the theme. If you're creating highly custom themes, you'll be spending a lot of time doing tweaks, making this method less passive and more of a side hustle.

39. Earn Reverse Passive Income with Trim

Reverse passive income is when you save money on something you were spending money on, therefore giving yourself more money than you had before.

The app Trim saves you money by negotiating your cable, internet, and phone bills, as well as attempting to negate bank fees, lower credit card APR, and cancel your unused subscriptions. For this service, you pay Trim a small portion of your first year's savings that they get you.

Trim reports that the average user saves hundreds of dollars, which means if you are the average user, you'll earn hundreds of dollars of reverse passive income by saving money with Trim.

You can check out Trim at:

https://cleancutfinance.com/asktrim

Risk involved: 10: Trim only charges you a portion of what you save, meaning if the app fails to save you money, then you don't pay anything.

Return: 1: Trim states the average user saves a few hundred dollars a year as a result of their service. While this may not seem like a ton, this form of reverse passive income takes minimal effort.

Feasibility: 10: Just about anyone can try out Trim.

Liquidity: 10: No money is locked up with this passive income method.

How Passive: 9: You may need to get on a phone call with Trim as they help you negotiate some of your bills. Otherwise, this method is almost entirely passive.

40. BE A SILENT BUSINESS PARTNER

Silent business partners invest financially in a company while allowing a partner to take care of daily operations.

You'll receive a portion of the profits regularly because you own a portion of the company. Many companies, especially startups, seek funding, and some will give partial ownership of their company in exchange for this funding, which will allow you to earn passive income without having to run a business.

Risk involved: 1: When you're a silent business partner, much of the ownership of the company is in your hands, meaning you're generally putting up quite a sum of capital to be involved.

Return: 10: Your potential return when you're a silent business partner is limitless, as you'll continually collect money as the business grows and flourishes.

Feasibility: 3: Finding a business opportunity and having the capital to get involved may be tricky, but that said, a lucrative opportunity awaits the patient and informed investor.

Liquidity: 5: Getting out of a business situation may be challenging as you'll need to sell off your portion of the business, which isn't always easy.

How Passive: 10: As a silent partner, your money does the work, not you, so this method is almost entirely passive.

41. RENT OUT YOUR STUFF

This passive income idea involves renting your stuff out online. You can do this on the site FriendWithA.

You'll take pictures of whatever is you want to rent and then create an ad online. Everyday things to rent out to people in the area include:

- Furniture
- Laptops
- Lawn care equipment
- Kitchenware

You can certainly rent out just about anything, which can be a great source of mostly passive income.

Risk involved: 9: The financial risk involved with renting out your stuff is the risk that your stuff will be damaged or stolen.

Return: 3: You may not make a killing out of renting your stuff, but it can be pretty easy money for just a little bit of work creating an ad and speaking with renters.

Feasibility: 10: Anyone who lives in an area where

renting stuff online is common can do this method.

Liquidity: 10: Money isn't tied up with this method.

How Passive: 8: You'll need to create ads for your stuff and deal with renters as they pick up and drop things off.

WRAPPING IT UP

————— ⚜ —————

A nd there you have it! 41 ways that you can start transforming your life by creating passive income. Remember, it often pays to focus on one income stream at a time and then branch out to other streams later. Find one that makes the most sense to you and that you feel the most comfortable with.

Thank you for purchasing Passive Income Made Simple!

Check out https://cleancutfinance.com to learn more about saving and making money to forge the path to a brighter future.

Made in the USA
Las Vegas, NV
23 February 2022

44453713R00059